Chiang Mai Stories

Adventures in Thailand

By Granville Kirkup

Copyright

Chiang Mai Stories: Adventures in Thailand

First edition, October 2016

Rimping Publishing Company

Cover design by The Illustrated Author

www.theillustratedauthor.net

Contents

FORWARD

While I am best known in Thailand for my books 'Thai Insider Chiang Mai', the definitive Chiang Mai guide book, and 'Chiang Mai: The Top 10', there is much more to Chiang Mai and Thailand than can be written in a guide book – interesting real stories of life in Thailand.

I have been a Chiang Mai visitor for thirty years and a part-time resident for ten years, and have run into some fascinating people and situations. You will meet many of these people in the twenty short stories in this book. They are all based on actual events, but of course some of the names have been changed to protect the innocent - and the not so innocent!

My thanks are due to Michael Toon and Don Burnell for sharing their Chiang Mai experiences with me over the years, and as always to my friend, the writer Robert Wisehart, for helping me to stop confusing British and American English!

Granville Kirkup

1: Jeff Dates a Bar Girl

Jeff was a British friend of ours from Walsall, near Birmingham. He would come to Thailand for his annual vacation, or for a 'holiday' as he would say. He was single and about 35 years old, and loved the easy life with the bar girls in Pattaya and Chiang Mai to entertain every night.

In Chiang Mai he met a bar girl called Jum, from a small village in the hills nearby. He liked that she was shy and not very pushy. He met her in a bar on Loi Kroh street – the 'bar street' - and bought her lady drinks. Lady drinks were for the girls who worked in the bar and cost 100 baht ($3). She received 20 baht from each drink as part of her wages.

The second night after a few drinks Jum said, "You big strong man Jeff", making a rude gesture with her hand. "Me go back hotel with you?"

That was fine with Jeff. They had a few more drinks and he paid her 'bar fine' to take her out of the bar and back to his hotel. Afterwards he paid her some money and sent her home.

The next night Jum was waiting for him at the bar, made it clear that he was 'hers' again for the evening, and warned off any other girl who tried to talk to Jeff. He found this quite flattering. Jum obviously liked him a lot.

This went on for several days and he gave Jum money every day. Sometimes he would have preferred to be with other bar girls, but Jum was always there. He went to another bar one night, and he had a good time. But when he got back to his hotel, Jum was waiting for him in the lobby.

"Mr Jeff!" she said angrily. "Why you no see me tonight? You no love me any more?" She was raising her voice and starting to cry.

He tried to calm her down and quickly walked her to his room. She was still crying.

"Yes, I love you", he said, "I was out with my friends." He reached into his wallet and gave her the usual money. "I will see you tomorrow night. You go home now."

"If you no want me to go with man from bar you must give me money", she said. I send money to family."

So that's how it went. He saw her almost every night, and even when she didn't come back to the hotel he gave her the same money.

She would often say to him, "Me no want work in bar and go with man any more", but she was always happy to take his money.

He was due to leave in a couple of days and return to England. They met in the bar for the last time.

"I will miss you Jum", he said.

"I miss you more long time", she replied. "When you come back?"

"Next year for sure. I will look for you."

"I no want to work in the bar any more. I love you. You send me money and I not work in bar and not see men."

"How would I send you money?"

"You can send to my bank." She pulled out an envelope on which someone had written the name 'Bangkok Bank' in English, a Swift code, an account number, and her real name in full. Something like Suramee Wanaporn. Jum could not write English so she was obviously well prepared for this eventuality.

"You would not work in the bar if I send you money?"

"No, I work hotel. I love you too much!"

So he went home to Walsall and sent her money every month. He also wrote to her, but how would she understand what he wrote in English?

Eventually he received a letter in the mail. It was typed and in good English. Obviously she did not write it herself. It said that she loved him, and thank you for the money, and she was now working in a hotel. But she had some bad news. Her mother was sick and needed to see the doctor or she may die. So could Jeff please send her 10,000 baht more this time? (About $300). She signed off with love. It looked like a very professional job.

Jeff's friend Tom was just leaving for Chiang Mai, so he asked him to go to the hotel and see if Jum was there. If not, to go look in the bar.

Tom called Jeff back in a few days. He went to the hotel and Jum was not there, in fact they knew of no one called 'Jum' who had ever worked there. He went to the bar, and there was Jum as large as life, sitting with a German man in a baseball cap, laughing at his jokes. But he was talking in German!

Tom talked to another customer in the bar, an elderly British man, and told him what had happened. He laughed when he heard the 'mother is sick' story, and called it the oldest bar girl trick in the book. Jum probably had three or four men in different parts of the world sending her money every month. All wired to her bank account!

Needless to say, Jeff did not send Jum any more money. He wrote to her that he knew she was still working at the bar, and that made him angry, after everything that she had promised. He never heard from her again.

2: David Blamed for a Road Accident

Thai roads can often be dangerous because Thai drivers consider road signs and stop lights to be just a suggestion – to be observed when the mood strikes them.

So you see road accidents fairly often, usually involving someone falling off a motorbike.

This happened to David, a young friend of ours who was visiting from California. He rented a car, and was getting used to driving on the 'wrong' side of the road, on the left, as they do in Thailand. He and his girlfriend Aimee went out for the day to Mae Rim, to see the elephants and have lunch at the Four Seasons. Heading back to town in the early evening, they reached the moat road and were waiting at a traffic light. Suddenly a motor bike roared past them at speed trying to make the light, which was already red.

The motorbike driver saw that he was not going to make it, swerved to avoid a truck crossing in front of him, tipped the bike over and fell onto the road! He lay there for a while, obviously hurt. The traffic started to move again, going past the downed motorbike on both sides.

David was shocked and wanted to help. He pulled his car to one side, got out, told Aimee to wait in the car and ran over to help the injured man on the road. David helped him up, but the bike was badly damaged. After pulling the bike out of the road as far as they could, the guy sank to the ground on the side of the road, holding his arm and his hand, which was bleeding.

David asked, "Do you need doctor? Hospital?" But the man did not seem to speak any English, and kept holding his arm in the air in pain.

A cop arrived on a motorbike, parked his bike at the side of the road and walked over. He did not look happy.

"I saw this accident", said David, but the cop ignored him and walked over to the motorbike driver. They talked heatedly in Thai, with the motorbike driver pointing at David. He sounded angry.

This went on for some time before the cop walked over to David, got out a notebook and pen and asked "You have license?"

David got out his wallet and produced a California driver's license, which is valid in Thailand.

The cop looked at it and wrote something in his notebook in Thai. This took quite a while, as he was copying from the license into his notebook.

Then came the bombshell, "You must pay for damage to motorbike."

David was shocked. What was going on?

"No you don't understand. I was just here to help. I was not involved in the accident!" He looked over at the motorbike driver, but the man just shrugged his shoulders and looked away.

The cop looked blankly at David, who tried to simplify things, "Me not in accident. Me just witness. Not my fault!"

The cop wrote '3000' in his notebook and showed it to David. "You pay damage. You pay three thousand baht."

"No!" replied David. "Not my fault! I not pay!"

The cop repeated "Three thousand baht. You pay now or come to police station!"

"Police station?" said David. This was getting more serious by the minute.

After watching all of this from the car, David's girlfriend Aimee got out and started yelling, first at the motorbike driver and then at the cop. "He was just trying to help. This is terrible!"

David tried to calm her down, and they discussed what to do. Three thousand baht is about $100 and they could afford that, but why should they pay at all? On the other hand a trip to the police station didn't sound good, when they didn't know the language, and perhaps they would get into more trouble.

Reluctantly they decided to pay. David pulled out three 1,000 baht notes from his wallet and handed them over to the cop. No receipt was offered. The cop and the motorbike driver conferred for a minute, but David couldn't see the money changing hands to the injured motorbike driver.

And that was it. They drove off and left the damaged motorbike, motorbike driver and the cop on the side of the road.

We saw David and Aimee the next day. They were very upset of course. We explained "This is Thailand and these things happen." We told them that if you see an accident in Thailand the best thing to do as a farrang (westerner) is to not get involved, because they think that a farrang is rich and can pay, so as much as you want to help, you have to leave things to the Thais and drive on!

3: Doug Fakes a Heart Attack, and Val Storms Off!

Doug and Val had been coming to Chiang Mai for a number of years. They were a couple in their 60s from Knutsford in Cheshire, and always came to get away from the cold British winters. He was a retired publican (pub owner) and they lived on a budget, but Doug was always the first to put his hand in his pocket to buy you a drink in the bar. I liked them both.

Markets are very popular in Chiang Mai, the Night Bazaar in particular: hundreds of stalls set up around Chang Klan Road in the middle of town, from about 5pm to midnight every night. They sell local handicrafts, fake designer goods, copy watches, clothing, silk and spices.

Bargaining is normal. You ask 'How much?' and the stallholder tells you in his limited English or get out a large calculator and enters a price. He may not know how to say the price in English, and you probably can't counter offer in Thai, so he hands you the calculator. You smile briefly and enter a lower price. It's usual to offer a price that is about half to two thirds of what is asked, and you end up around two thirds to three quarters.

For some reason, the normal method of bargaining in the market was not for Doug and Val! Doug was always looking for a bargain, and his opinion of the market was that they were 'foreigners' who would rip you off if they possibly could!

So he typically approached a stall holder with something he might want to buy and ask "How much is this?"

The stallholder might reply "One thousand baht."

At this Doug would double up in pain and fake a heart attack, holding onto his chest with one hand and waving the other in the air in panic.

"One thousand baht!   I thought you said *one thousand baht*!", he would cry, by now almost dropping to the ground.

By this point, a small crowd might gather to see what was going on, while the stall holder worried about all the commotion.

Doug always recovered sufficiently to spit out "I give you three hundred baht! Very good price for you!" They would end up somewhere in the middle, by now Doug effecting a miraculous recovery.

I saw this happen many times, and it always seemed to work. Another ploy he often used was "How much for two?"   And getting a lower price for two items, he expected me to buy one of them.

Val on the other hand had a completely different technique. She would walk up to the unsuspecting stallholder with something she was interested in, and ask "How much is this?"

The stallholder might reply "Eight hundred baht."

"Eight hundred baht?" Val would scream, "You must be bloody joking!" and she would storm off.

As a bargaining technique this left much to be desired, because she would never actually buy anything! One time I decided to step in, and after she screamed "Eight hundred baht!" I got out a five hundred baht note and passed it over to the stall holder, who accepted it gratefully. I never found out whether Val was grateful though, I don't think she really wanted to buy, and she never paid me back!

4: Granville and the Orphanage

My wife Sidney and I were living in Chiang Mai one winter and we met a British guy, Tony, who was involved with the church.

He would often help out with a Catholic orphanage, and said that they had plans to expand. He invited us to go with him one weekend to take a look.

"I really want you to see what they are doing there," he said. "They are hoping to build a new computer classroom."

I am a retired computer programmer so I said, "That's great. We would love to help with that."

We are not church people, but agreed to go, and set off with Tony in the car. It was a good distance away, a couple of hours beyond Mae Rim, in a small village beside a river.

We arrived at the orphanage to discover that it was not run by nuns, as we had imagined, but by a Catholic family. Tony introduced us to Mark, who was in charge. He welcomed us, offered us soft drinks, and we started a tour.

With children varying in age from toddlers to teenagers, and with both girls and boys the orphanage consisted of a fairly large piece of land, with several buildings, including a bathroom block. Two of the buildings were dormitories for the children, and they looked well cared for.

We noticed that the dormitories had bibles here and there and Christian crosses on the walls. This surprised us because Thailand is a Buddhist country, and we did not see the benefit of bringing up the children as Catholics. However this was a Catholic orphanage, after all, so what did we expect?

"Now let me show you the plans for our new computer classroom," said Mark proudly. He unrolled a professional plan of a new building, with desks and Internet wiring.

"That is most impressive," we said, "and it will be a great benefit to the children."

He nodded along as we said this as if expecting us to say a lot more, although we weren't sure exactly what.

"How many computers are you planning to have," I asked.

"That depends on what sort of funding we can raise." He replied. "We would like ten or fifteen."

The tour took a couple of hours. We thanked them and prepared to leave. Thinking ahead, I had brought some money with us to make a donation, and I gave Mark seven thousand baht, which was about $200. I thought this was quite generous considering that we are not wealthy, but everyone seemed to awkwardly stand around while Mark looked at us strangely until we left.

We did not hear from anyone connected with the orphanage again, nor did we ever hear from Tony. We didn't know what we had done wrong until a mutual friend told us that Tony told the orphanage people that we would probably be willing to pay for the new computer classroom and all of the computers to go with it!

We understood now. They were disappointed. So were we. No one likes being taken for granted.

5: Guy and the Lady Boy Surprise

What follows happened to several first time visitors to Chiang Mai who we know, but for convenience we will call all of these guys 'Guy'.

In one case, Guy was a hapless young man from Scotland, who thought that his first visit to Thailand would be all fun and sex. That may be true if you go to the Patpong area of Bangkok, or Walking Street in Pattaya, but in Chiang Mai there are few 'girly' bars – just a couple of Go-Go bars around the town and some hostess bars on Loi Kroh Street – the bar street between the moat and the Night Bazaar.

Guy was going to a restaurant one night and tried to get a tuk tuk to take him there. The tuk tuk driver said "One hundred baht".

Guy said, "No, too much!   I give you eighty baht."

They haggled over this for a minute or two, and agreed that ninety baht would be a fair price.

When we met Guy later, he told us proudly how he had knocked down the tuk tuk driver from 100 baht to 90 baht, saying, "He was trying to rip me off!"

We pointed out that the ten baht reduction was only 30 cents or 20p!

Another time, Guy decided that a songthaew (red truck) would be cheaper than a tuk tuk,, so he stopped one, gave his destination and asked "How much?" The driver looked surprised, and said "Fifty baht".

So when Guy got out he gave the driver fifty baht and walked away feeling quite pleased. When he told us about this, we explained that you don't ask the price when taking a songthaew. The price is always twenty baht, anywhere in town. When you get out you just give the driver twenty baht and you are done.

Thai massage is another source of confusion. Young men like Guy often see a sign for 'Thai massage' and think, 'Woo hoo! Happy ending!' Unfortunately for them this is not the case. Thai massage takes place with all of your clothes on (or a loose fitting robe), and they bend you and contort you. It's an acquired taste and can be quite painful.

The other type of massage, which Guy was probably looking for, is called 'body massage', and takes place naked. Sometimes the girl will be naked too. There are not many body massage places in Chiang Mai.

One night Guy was visiting bars on Loi Kroh road and went into the Boxing Stadium Complex, an area of many bars near an arena for Thai kick boxing. He picked out a bar with the best looking girls, some in evening dresses, and ordered a drink.

A girl came over and talked to him. She said her name was Nok, and after a few minutes she said "You buy me one drink?" Buying a girl a 'lady drink' is the accepted way of giving her a tip when she is sitting with you.

He bought her a drink, then another, and they played pool for a while. She was certainly one of the prettiest girls he had seen in Chiang Mai.

They sat down again with more drinks, and Nok leaned over seductively and said to him, "You want me to come back your hotel? We have fun!"

He couldn't believe his luck, and quickly paid the 'bar fine' so that she could leave the bar.

They got a tuk tuk back to his hotel, and she went up to his room. "I shower now", she said, "Then you shower!"

She seemed shy and undressed with a towel around her, showered, and got into bed. Still with the towel wrapped tightly around her.

He showered and got into bed naked. This was going to be fun! He felt her hands on him, and started to explore her body, the towel now gone. His hand strayed between her legs. But what was this? His hand felt … well, let's just say it wasn't what he expected!

He shot out of bed, and yelled "You are a man!"

"Yes, I am ladyboy!" Nok replied. "You not know? I thought you liked me!" She started to cry, but Guy didn't know whether this was part of the show.

Guy dressed quickly and pointed at Nok's clothes to get her to leave. She still expected money so Guy reluctantly opened his wallet and gave her five hundred baht ($15). She left quickly, presumably to go back to the bar and give another customer a Ladyboy Surprise!

On a more successful evening a girl called Nang was getting ready to leave Guy's hotel room late at night. "How much should I give you?" he asked her.

"Up to you!" she replied, so he gave her two thousand baht ($60). She pouted a little at that, and seemed to be upset. "And you give me money for motorbike taxi!" she demanded. He gave her another hundred baht and hoped she would leave quickly.

She walked over to the hotel room minibar. "And you give me one drink?" she asked.

He hoped she was leaving but he said "Yes, OK."

Nang opened her bag and scooped every small bottle from the mini bar into it – vodka, gin, whisky, rum, sodas. Then she stormed out, and slammed the door behind her.

Guy was certainly more careful with bar girls in future!

6: Carol Gets an American Visa

Carol Martin and her husband ran several five star hotels in Thailand. They also owned a chain of restaurants and employed several thousand Thai people. Although born in New York, she had lived in Thailand for all her adult life, and eventually became a Thai citizen.

That was important in Thailand, where it's much easier for Thai citizens to own businesses and property, but it was a problem for her when she wanted to return to the US for her occasional visits. In that case, like any Thai citizen, she had to get an American visa to make the trip. That may seem unusual for someone who was born in America, but that's the way that it works.

I was introduced to Carol by a mutual friend at her restaurant in Chiang Mai, and she told us this story.

She made an appointment with the US embassy in Bangkok to apply for an American visa. After a long wait, she was ushered into a private office and interviewed by a young American man in a suit.

"Would you like this interview to be conducted in Thai or English?" he asked.

"Either is fine. I speak both. English then."

"What is your purpose in wishing to visit the United States?" he asked.

"To visit friends and family."

"And how long do you wish to visit?"

"Er, about three weeks," she replied.

"Who will be paying for your trip and your expenses while you are there?"

"I will... or my husband."

"Which one of those is it?"

"Well, I will. I have money. It will not be a problem."

"Now let me ask you some questions about your lifestyle," he said. "Have you ever been a prostitute?"

She was astonished. "No of course not!" she replied.

There were several more personal questions in a similar vein. Then he asked "What do you do for a living?"

"My husband and I are in the hotel and restaurant business."

"You mean you have a bar with rooms for rent above?" he asked.

This was getting too much. "No, we own all of the .... Hotels in Thailand," she said quite loudly, mentioning the well-known hotel name.

He looked shocked and embarrassed at this new information, stood up, and left the room without saying another word.

She waited in the interview room for another few minutes, and then a senior looking American woman came in and sat down opposite her, looking flustered.

"Mrs Martin?" she said, "I'm Pamela Ewes, the head of the visa section. Did you have dinner with the American Ambassador just last night?"

"Oh yes we did. He was the guest of my husband and I."

"I am so sorry, Mrs Martin," said Pamela. "Your visa has been approved and will be ready tomorrow."

7: Don and the Rusty Nail

I was born in England but have lived in the US for many years, when not in Thailand. Don, my late brother-in-law lived in England, and once a year we would meet in Chiang Mai for our two-week vacation, or 'holiday' as he called it.

We would often go to The Riverside, a bar and restaurant on the banks of the Ping River, near the Nawarat Bridge. The Riverside was larger in those days, there were basically two large wooden buildings on the river frontage, and at night there would be a different band in each building.

Don and I liked to go to the Riverside for dinner and then sit at the bar afterwards and watch one of the bands. We always sat at the long bar, never at a table, and we got to know the bands that played there.

Our barman was a young man called Lor, and one day we asked him, "Do you know how to make a Rusty Nail?" I had learned of that drink at a 'grand hotel' bar on a trip to Europe the year before.

"Lusty Nail?" he said.

Obviously, he had not heard of it, so I gave him instructions – Johnny Walker Black Label scotch whisky,

Drambuie and ice. It took a few evenings to get the mixture just right – less Drambuie than whisky, and lots of ice, but soon he was making both of us a 'Lusty Nail' as soon as we sat down each night.

Don was a heavy smoker in those days, and a couple of years later developed throat cancer and had to have a tracheotomy. He was back in Thailand the following year, and had a characteristic way of touching the valve in his throat when he talked. He quit smoking, but still drank Rusty Nails any chance he could.

We went to see Lor at the Riverside. "What happen you?" he said, indicating the valve in Don's throat.

"Too much smoking," said Don, making a smoking sign with his hand. As his illness progressed he had to use sign language a lot more.

We annually went back to Chiang Mai for about another ten years and Don did OK, though he was getting weaker each year and unable to walk very far. Finally, and sadly, he passed away from throat cancer when in England.

I went to see Lor at the Riverside on my next Chiang Mai trip. 'Our' half of the Riverside had been torn down to make way for a new restaurant, and Lor was now the barman of the Craft Beer Factory, over the road. He said "Where your friend?" touching his throat in a way that Don would.

I told him that Don was with us no more, but ordered a Rusty Nail for old time's sake.

When I got home I had some cards made entitled 'How to make a Rusty Nail' with a photo of Black Label scotch whisky, Drambuie and ice on the front, and a photo of Don and I at the bar at the Riverside, Rusty Nails in hand, and Lor standing proudly behind us.

Don is long gone now, but not forgotten.

8: Jiab and the Monks

This story took place in Birmingham, England, but I include it here because it has Chiang Mai connections.

Tom was about fifty years old and involved in the sale of restaurants and pubs in England. He lived in a big house in Sutton Coldfield, on the outskirts of Birmingham, with his Thai wife Jiab. Jiab was about 30 and from Bangkok, but they met in Chiang Mai where Tom had a second home, which is where I met him.

Tom drove a Bentley with a personalized number plate showing his initials, TEO 1, Thomas Edward Ormerod 1. Let me tell you about personal number plates in England. You cannot order them from the car licensing authority as you can in the U.S., you have to buy an existing number plate from someone who already has it, or from a car number plate dealer. 'Cherished' number plates, as they are called, can change hands for tens of thousands of pounds. You cannot have number plates with words, but you can sometimes find a combination of letters and numbers that looks like a word. For example, a famous comedian had COM 1C, which he made into COMIC. That must have cost a good deal.

Tom was delighted with his personal number plate, but one day as they were having lunch in a Birmingham restaurant, Jiab raised the subject.

"I love my car", she said, "But some of my friends have personal plates with their initials. Why can't I have that too? Like you do?"

"But I just bought you a new Mercedes!" he said. He was surprised and a bit upset.

"I know, and I like it a lot. But can't you get me "Thai Gal' or something like that? Something fun?"

'You can't get words like that on a number plate. You have to buy a plate that someone already has. It's just luck if you can make a word out of it, and that would cost a lot."

"But you are lucky! Get my initials then!"

"Why aren't you satisfied with your nice Mercedes? What did you drive when I met you? A motorbike?"

Jiab was upset by this outburst and they hardly spoke for the rest of the day. So Tom thought he has better see about getting her a personal plate. He looked at the lists of number plates for sale in the Sunday Times, as he often did, but did not find Jiab's initials. So he contacted a number plate dealer who advertised in the newspaper, and gave them Jiab's full name.

A few weeks later he received a call from the dealer. "Mr Ormerod?" the caller said, "We think we have found you a very good number plate. It is J1 ABS"

"J1 ABS?" he replied. "But those are not her initials."

"No, if you put that together on a plate it will make JIABS!"

Tom was amazed, this was even better than he had hoped. He paid the fifteen thousand pounds, and registered the plate for Jiab's car. Her birthday was coming up in a few days, so on her birthday he secretly had the new plates fitted to her car. She was shocked and delighted, and couldn't believe that he actually found her name! This was even better than her girlfriends! Now she felt bad that she'd been upset with him earlier.

They often went to the Buddhist temple in Birmingham so that Jiab could make merit, and the next time they went they drove there in her Mercedes.

After making a donation of fruit, flowers and cash, they talked to the head monk. He was from Chiang Mai and they knew him well, so they proudly took him outside to see the Mercedes with the JIABS number plate.

"What do you think?" asked Tom, winking at Jiab.

"Yes, that is very good," replied the monk, "To have your name on the car like that. Could you get me a number plate too?"

Tom was a bit surprised, because monks take a vow of poverty. "They are expensive, but I could look into it for you," he said.

"There are three monks here in the temple," said the monk, "So please will you get us MONK 1, MONK 2 and MONK 3?"

As Tom said later, "It's a good think there weren't ten monks in the temple!"

9: Katie Almost Visits The Oriental

Once or twice during our three month stay in Chiang Mai every winter we make a side trip to Bangkok, where we stay at the Mandarin Oriental. A hotel which was known for years simply as 'The Oriental' and that is the name that we still use. (Similarly, we always refer to Myanmar as 'Burma' – we prefer the old names!)

Several years ago we were planning a trip to Bangkok when our young friends Katie and Susan from Wyoming told us that they would be in Bangkok at the same time.

"We have to get together," we said. "Why don't you come and meet us at the Oriental?"

They were traveling on a budget, so we thought that drinks and dinner at the Oriental, a five-star hotel, would be a welcome change for them.

The date came and they called us, saying "Where is your hotel? Our guest house is off Sukhumvit, how do we get there?"

This was not a good start. The Oriental is on all maps of Bangkok. We told them to use a taxi or tuk tuk, or the Sky Train, which has a stop a few hundred yards from the Oriental at Taksin Bridge.   We arranged to meet them in the Bamboo Bar at the hotel at 7pm for drinks.

7pm came and went, then 7:30. Then about 8pm there was a call on my cell phone.

"It's me!" said Katie, "Oh my God! We eventually found The Oriental but they would not let us in!"

"What do you mean?" I asked. "They wouldn't let you in? Why not?"

"They were very polite about it, but they said it's because we are not hotel guests and we're both carrying backpacks and wearing shorts."

"Oh no!" I replied, "You brought *backpacks* to the Oriental?"

It was part of the dress code at this old-established hotel that no shorts were allowed in the evening and no backpacks ever, except maybe if you were a guest in your hotel returning to your room.

"We didn't want to leave our backpacks at our small guest house," she said.

"Where are you now?" I asked.

"We are at the Royal Orchid Sheraton down the street. They were fine with us coming in here!"

So we walked the half mile or so to the Sheraton and she was right, it is a nice hotel. We had drinks and dinner there.   For ever more, Katie referred to this incident as 'The time we got thrown out of the Oriental!'

10: Granville's Car Gets Clamped

Driving in Thailand can be difficult, because Thai drivers – particularly on motorbikes – seem to think that the road laws are optional and do not apply to them.

But don't make the mistake, as I did, of thinking that you can get away with anything on the road that you please.

I went for an acupuncture treatment one day, at a clinic on a busy road on the inside of the moat – the old town in Chiang Mai, where parking is always at a premium. Despite driving up and down several streets, I found nowhere to park. Eventually I found a parking space near the entrance to a side road with plenty of room for my car without causing any obstruction, but the curb was painted with a red and white check, which in Thailand means 'No Parking'.

I thought it over for a few moments and concluded, "What are they going to do? Give me a ticket?" I drive on an American license in Thailand, not a Thai license.

So I parked at the red and white curb and walked away to my acupuncture appointment, looking back at the car a little guiltily.

An hour later I was done with my appointment and walked back to the car. It was still where I had parked it, but now it bore a big yellow clamp on one of the front wheels. In my driver's side window was a sign in Thai and English, saying that my car had been clamped for illegal parking, and was not to be driven. There was also a numbered white ticket.

Not sure what to do, I walked into a local shop holding both the sign and the ticket. "My car was clamped," I said. "I go police station?"

They got the idea, though their English was as limited as my Thai. They said, "Go tuk tuk police station."

But which police station and where was it? I hailed a passing tuk tuk and showed the driver my clamped car and the sign. He said 'One hundred baht,' so I assumed he knew where I should go.

I got in and we drove off. Ten minutes later we pulled into a police station by the river and the flower market, and the tuk tuk driver pointed the way inside.

It was all in Thai, but I held up the clamping sign and ticket and was shown into a large waiting room. I took a number from a machine. Numbers were being shouted out every few minutes in Thai, and though my Thai is very limited, I do know Thai numbers because it helps with shopping.

They read out 'Ha Jet', which is 57, and I was 'Jet Sam' or 73, so I would have quite a wait. It turned out to be about an hour. Finally 'Jet Sam' was called and I made my way to the desk. Two officers in uniform were sitting behind the desk. They took my ticket and asked me for five hundred baht ($15) in quite good English, and gave me a receipt in Thai.

I wondered how to get my car back, and as if in response, one of the officers picked up a hand radio and made a call, referring to the numbers on my ticket as he did so.

"You go back to car now", he said.

So after some delay I found a tuk tuk outside. I had some difficulty explaining where I wanted to go, but fortunately I knew the road name for the acupuncture clinic, so I went there.

I walked from the clinic back to my car, and was just in time to see a motorcycle cop removing the clamp.

I did get my car back, and all was fine, but it had taken me over three hours for the whole process. Lesson learned. I always parked legally in Thailand after that!

11: Paul's Marriage Shock

Paul was a friend of mine from England, a London businessman importing inexpensive electronic gadgets from Taiwan and Hong Kong. He went through a messy divorce and had to pay his ex-wife a lot of money, but he kept the business and eventually sold it to a Russian for over a million pounds.

Paul liked Thai girls and he knew that I often went to Thailand. For his first trip, he accompanied me to Bangkok, then went many times to Pattaya and Chiang Mai on his own. He was not interested in bar girls. He wanted to find a respectable Thai girl that he could court and maybe one day marry.

He was in Chiang Mai one day buying a pair of reading glasses at an optician's shop where he was served by a pretty Thai girl in her 20s. He asked her name. She said it was Lek.

"This is my uncle's shop and I am helping him," she said. "I live in Bangkok."

He was impressed with Lek and her good English. She was obviously not a bar girl. He found every reason he could to go back to the shop several times: adjust his glasses: try on new glasses: get an eye test. Each time he made sure that Lek was there, and that she served him.

Eventually he plucked up the courage to ask her if she would meet him for a drink, after work.

She looked shocked, and giggled behind her hand. "Cannot!" she said, "I am Buddhist and do not drink."

"Oh OK, well just coffee then?"

"Cannot. I cannot see a man on my own. I must have friend with me. I think the word is 'chaperone'!"

He left it at that, but the next day he decided to go back and try again.

"OK, so you bring a chaperone and we can go for coffee, or dinner."

"I think you are a good man," she said. "You have seen me in the shop many times. I talked to my auntie about you. She said that if you ask me again, she will be chaperone and I can see you."

They went out several times, first for coffee and later for dinner, always with the aunt tagging along as a chaperone.

Paul got to know Lek's aunt and uncle in Chiang Mai very well, and they saw him as a suitable suitor for Lek. It is the ambition of many Thai girls to marry a wealthy western man, so this was not so unusual.

But what about her parents in Bangkok?

"OK, I have met your aunt and uncle", said Paul, "If I am to see more of you perhaps I should meet your parents?"

Meeting a girl's parents may seem an unusual or outdated way to get a date, but that is the polite Thai way.

"Yes", agreed Lek, "I think that would be best."

So Paul arranged for a flight to Bangkok, with Lek and her aunt, to go and meet Lek's parents. They had dinner at a nice Italian restaurant (Paul was trying to show off) and they got along fine. Lek's dad knew a little English and Lek translated for her mom.

"Now we all go for karaoke!" announced Dad.

Karaoke in Thailand is an excuse to drink a lot in a bar, which they did. Lek's dad sang some Sinatra songs fairly well, and Paul had a go at one, too. Sometimes in Thai karaoke your bar hostess (usually a nicely dressed young girl) will sing the songs for you, so you don't have to get up and do it yourself!

Paul seemed to meet with Lek's parents' approval, so when they got back to Chiang Mai he asked her if she would like to go to the island of Koh Samui for three days with him.

"Sure", replied Lek. "We go with my auntie and I sleep in her room."

Once again, that was the polite Thai way. The courtship continued like this for some time until there was an engagement ceremony in a hotel in Chiang Mai. For this Paul had to 'display his wealth' to show that he was a suitable suitor for Lek. He put gold and piles of baht on a table surrounded by flowers.

After that, Lek and Paul were able to go away together, but they were careful not to let Lek's parents know.

They were married six months later in a hotel in Bangkok, with the parents, aunts, uncles and other family members in attendance. Nine Buddhist monks officiated at the wedding. I went to both the engagement party and the wedding.

They had planned to live in Chiang Mai, so they looked at a western style house near Hang Dong, with a surrounding wall, swimming pool, a two car garage, and room for live-in servants. Paul was very proud of his new Thai wife, and of his new house. He often invited friends from England to visit and stay with them.

But then things started to go downhill. Paul was 20 years older than Lek, chauvinistic and insecure. I was at his house one day and he told me he had to take Lek to the hairdressers. I wondered why, since they had two cars and Lek could easily drive.

When she was out of the room, he explained. "I have to take her to the hairdressers because I don't want her talking to any men!"

He also didn't want her going out with any girlfriends, presumably because they might talk to men, and neither did he want her girlfriends to come over to the house because they would talk in Thai, and he didn't understand what they were talking about.

Yes, he was very controlling. Worse, he saw nothing wrong with it.

Lek was depressed by his treatment of her and would sometimes go and stay with her parents in Bangkok, just to get away.

A year passed, and then things suddenly went from bad to worse. Paul and Lek were in Bangkok staying at the JW Marriott when Paul had a stroke. He was rushed to the Bumungrad hospital for tests, which did not go well. The outcome was that he lost the use of one of his legs and was confined to a wheelchair.

He was back home in a week or so, but now it was his turn to be depressed. It looked like his condition was permanent, so they sold one of the cars and bought Paul a motorized wheelchair. But he could only get around the house and grounds in the wheelchair, and then only on the ground floor. The upstairs was off-limits for the rest of his life.

Now positions were reversed. Lek went out whenever she wished and Paul could do nothing about it. They might go out together in the car, but it was difficult to take the wheelchair and maneuver him, so they rarely did. His friends visited, but his speech was now quite slurred and they visited less as time passed. I saw him from time to time, but he was very depressed and had little to say. We would email but he often lost track of what he had told me the day before.

A few months later, I was away in Bangkok and heard that he had died. It was not a surprise, but still sad. I was glad that I had seen him many times when he was alive and in better spirits.

And what of Lek? She inherited a new Mercedes, the big house in Hang Dong and the servants that went with it. I saw her not long after Paul died and she asked me if I would lend her a million baht to pay taxes. I refused and I never heard from her again. I hear that she now has a Thai boyfriend living in the big house, and they plan to get married.

This is a story that is often repeated in Thailand. An older western man marries a much younger Thai girl and gives her a good lifestyle but wants to control her. But then he dies and she gets everything!

12: Mr. Dan the Buddha Man and the Elephant

At the bottom of Tha Phae Road, around the corner from the Night Bazaar is the shop of Mr. Dan the Buddha Man. There are dozens of Buddha shops in Chiang Mai, but Mr. Dan's is different. As a sign in the shop proudly says, "All Buddhas blessed in the temple before sale."

That is enough for us. There is a move in Thailand against selling Buddhas for 'decoration', but Mr. Dan's promise that the Buddhas have been blessed in the temple is sufficiently reverent. When friends visit us in Chiang Mai we always take them to Mr. Dan's shop to look at Buddhas.

Sometimes our friends pick up small Buddhas and take them home, but if you buy a Buddha of any size – six to twelve inches high for example – it is better to ship it home. Mr. Dan takes care of that, and obtains the necessary permit. Unfortunately he has to ship by sea, which takes two to three months.

We did this for our friend Pam from Dallas, another friend, Katie from California, and my daughter Louise, also from California. They all loved their Thai Buddhas, and 'Blessed in temple' made them more special.

We had two visitors from Charleston South Carolina, Harriett and her partner Cheryl. We took them on a walk around the town, as we usually do with visitors, including Mr. Dan's shop. They loved the Buddhas, but there was so much to look at they didn't decide to buy anything and we moved in to other stores.

A couple of weeks after they returned to Charleston, we received an email from Harriett.

"We have been thinking about the nice Buddha shop that you took us to, and now we are sorry that we didn't buy something," she said. "We are thinking of an elephant! But not a small one, a fairly large one. Could you have one shipped to us and we will send you the money for it?"

"OK, we can certainly do that," we replied. "But how large and what color and what material? You can get them in wood or resin, brown or black."

"Oh certainly a wooden elephant. Maybe about ten inches high, and light brown if you can get that," she emailed back

The next day we went back to Mr. Dan's shop and asked about an elephant. They had ten-inch high wooden elephants but they were black, and we really wanted brown. Mr. Dan was not in the shop so I talked to his assistant, holding a ten-inch high black wooden elephant and saying "Elephant same this but color brown!" and pointing to a much smaller brown elephant.

I think she got the idea, but said "No have big elephant brown", so we left disappointed.

The next day we returned to the shop, and this time Mr. Dan was there. We went through the "Want same elephant as this but in brown" procedure again, and he understood.

"Is no problem," he said, "We can make for you. You want elephant same this, made from wood, but color brown? We make."

"Yes", we agreed. With that, he worked out a price. Including shipping to Charleston it was about $100.

Harriett and Cheryl were delighted that we found them an elephant, and sent us a check when we got home to California. We told them that shipping might take two or even three months.

The months went by, two months, then three. No elephant. Harriett asked if we could contact Mr. Dan, but we were no longer in Chiang Mai, so there was no way to reach him. Of course we did not have a tracking number because the elephant had not been made when we ordered it. We thought of sending a friend in Chiang Mai to visit the shop and ask about the missing elephant.

After four months we heard from Harriett again. "It looks like we will not be getting our elephant then," she said.

We told her that three months is pretty normal, but in this case they had to make the elephant first, so how long would that take?   A month?   We wondered whether we should return her $100.

But two days later, we received an excited email from Harriett. "Guess what? Our elephant ARRIVED!   We just unpacked it and it is perfect!   It is so much better even than we had hoped! It's sitting here on our table!"

So Mr. Dan the Buddha man had once again saved the day!

13: Michael and the Roulette Nuns

Michael and Om lived in a big house in Mae Rim, on the outskirts of Chiang Mai. He was from Manchester and was a former professional poker player. She was from Bangkok, probably a bar girl in her past life but they never admitted it.

Married about ten years, Michael was a kind hearted rogue who had donated once or twice to a catholic orphanage nearby. One day two nuns from the orphanage, Sister Sarah and Sister Mary, came to the house asking for a donation. They explained that the nuns were building a school and needed money for books and supplies.

Michael was brought up the hard way and was not a pushover. Although he was quite well off, he earned his money and didn't like giving it away.

But as he listened to the nuns he came up with an idea.

"So how much do you need?" he asked.

"Whatever you can give," Sister Sarah replied. "The Lord will provide for us, but sometimes we need help!"

"So more than ten thousand baht?"

"That would be most generous, but we could certainly use more if you wish to give it."

Thinking about it for a moment, he asked "Would you be willing to take a gamble?"

"It is not in our nature to gamble. What do you mean?"

"Well, we are going to Macau tomorrow. As you know, there people gamble. Have you heard of roulette?"

"Yes, we have heard of it. A gambling game," Sister Sarah replied.

"Yes, you choose a number and they spin a wheel with a ball in it. If the ball lands in your number, you win thirty-five times the amount that you bet. Do you get the idea?"

"Yes?"

"Well, I would like to give you a donation, and bet that donation on a roulette number. Then if I win, you will get a lot more money."

"That sounds very good", she replied. "We are not gambling people, but if that's the way that you want to make a donation, then by all means go ahead."

"OK, then", said Michael, "We will go to Macau and put ten thousand baht on number. That's about three hundred dollars."

"Ten thousand baht? What number will you choose?"

"Number seventeen," Michael replied. "I always bet on number seventeen".

"And what time will you make this bet?"

"Shall we say 8 o'clock Chiang Mai time?"

"Very well then", she replied, "We will pray for you and ask for number seventeen to win at exactly eight o'clock in the evening."

"Thank you", said Michael, "Come back in a few days, after we return, and I will let you know how we did."

The next day, Michael and Om flew to Macau, and got themselves a very nice room at the Wynn. Michael was known as a high roller, so they didn't have to pay for the room. Michael passed the time playing poker while Om played the slots.

Approaching 8pm they went into the high limit tables room and asked for a private roulette table.

"Certainly we can arrange that sir", said the pit boss. "Is there anything else that you require?"

"Yes, I would like some holy water," he quipped. "No make that a gin and tonic. Then I have a special bet I wish to place at exactly 8 o'clock."

"Certainly sir", replied the pit boss.

Michael put down $300 for chips, and just before 8 o'clock he carefully placed all of the chips on number seventeen. He looked at his watch and asked the dealer to wait for a minute or two.

At exactly 8 o'clock he asked the dealer to commence play. The dealer spun the wheel, and spun the ball in the opposite direction. The little silver ball circled the wheel two or three times, bounced around... and landed directly in number seventeen!

"Well done sir!" said the dealer, "Number seventeen it is!"

"There was never a doubt!" Michael told the puzzled dealer, who paid out the $10,500 winnings while the pit boss nodded his approval.

Two days later they were back in Mae Rim. As planned, the nuns returned to the house. Michael had a big fat envelope waiting for them with over three hundred and fifty thousand baht in it, bound with two thick rubber bands.

The nuns were thrilled to receive such a large donation and were very grateful.

"Yes, the Lord works in mysterious ways", said Michael. "We can all use a little help, but it wasn't until that moment that I understood the power of prayer!"

14: Tawan the Dating Elephant

Some years ago my wife Sidney and I answered an appeal from The Elephant Foundation, a London-based nonprofit concerned with the welfare of elephants in Thailand and elsewhere. Their story was that, with a suitable small donation, you could 'date an elephant' and you would receive a letter from him or her.

So we applied, and we were put in touch with Tawan, a young male elephant who was injured in a road accident in Bangkok, and now lived in Chiang Rai.

We received a charming letter from Tawan. I no longer have that letter, but I remember it saying that we would love his 'charming swagger' and that he couldn't wait to meet us!

Sidney wrote back to Tawan, and this is what she said:

Dear Plai Tawan:

You are my big hero, and that charming swagger of yours does it for me!

I hope that you have been having lots of adventures, and can't wait to hear about them in your next letter.

Here in America, there are not many elephants. But I have been proud to name my car after you. My license plate reads 'TAWAN 1'.

All my love,

Sidney Kirkup

The next year we were in London, and we stopped by The Elephant Foundation to meet them at their offices. They were happy to see us, although they were busy writing elephant letters!

Several years later we were living at our home in Chiang Mai, and we wondered if we could actually meet Tawan. We found out that the main elephant camp in Chiang Rai was based in the grounds of the Anantara Hotel, with the same ownership as the Four Seasons Tented Camp next door, a place we had always wanted to visit.

We booked a few days at The Four Seasons Tented Camp in Chiang Rai, although we wondered how to get there, as there are no flights between Chiang Mai and Chiang Rai. If you want to fly, you would have to go via Bangkok to make the journey. Traveling by car, it's about a four hour road trip between Chiang Mai and Chiang Rai. I am fine driving in Thailand, but this didn't appeal to me. However the Four Season Tented Camp manager told us that if we drove to the Four Seasons Resort in Chiang Mai, and leave our car there, their driver would take us to Chiang Rai in a minibus.

And that is what we did. We had a very nice morning drive with a Thai driver, and we stopped for a picnic along the way.

We checked into the Tented Camp – not really tents as they have a wooden floor and a bathroom, but if they want to call that a tent that is fine with me.

We talked to the manager again, "Do you really have an elephant here called Tawan? A young male who was rescued from Bangkok we think."

He smiled at that, and said he would find out and let us know.

The next morning we were sitting having breakfast on the patio when a group of young elephants were brought over to meet us by their mahouts. One in particular caught our eye – they usually bring females to breakfast because they are more docile, but this was a young male with tusks – it was Tawan!

They all laughed and said, "Of course we know Tawan! He is a little rogue! Only last week he escaped and crossed over the river into Burma!"

We said our hellos to Tawan and had our picture taken with him. We gave him the freshest bunch of bananas that we could find!

Later we went to see where Tawan lived at the elephant compound at Anantara next door, and met his mahout.

Each mahout takes care of one elephant, and they often have a lifelong relationship together.

Anantara not only takes care of the elephants, they take care of the mahout and the mahout's family, teaching them weaving and other skills, so they can make an income.

We were sorry that we could no longer date Tawan, as they no longer wrote those letters, but we were pleased to see how well he was doing, and that he was happily living in Chiang Mai. We plan to go back and see him again before too long!

15: Sandra Decides to Come Out

Sandra was a neighbor of our friends Alam and Bill at the Peak Condo off Chang Klan Road. She was a graphic designer, mostly creating book covers for self-published books. You are not allowed to work in Thailand as a farrang (westerner), but she worked at home on the Internet and people paid her by Paypal. So by not actually working for a Thai company she got away with it.

She was from Solihull in England, as she used to say, 'Where Range Rovers are made.' She was about 50 and lived in Thailand for almost 20 years, at first in Chiang Mai with her husband. But he became interested in Thai girls and eventually moved to Bangkok where he married a much younger Thai girl.

So Sandra was on her own, but kept busy with her work. We often asked her over for drinks on our balcony, or out to dinner at the Riverside, a local restaurant.

She often complained, "It's terrible here being a western woman of my age. Western men come here for Thai girls, who are always available because they are looking for western men to provide for them. I love the weather here, but it's useless for sex!"

She had many gay men friends and even went on trips with them. One year she went on her own to Malaysia and was shocked that a Malaysian guide she met offered to "Give you sexy massage madam!" She later discovered that was popular with certain German lady tourists.

Another time she had a male visitor from Oregon come to stay with her. We wondered if 'romance may be in the air', but she told us that the first things he wanted to do were to go for a body massage and then meet young Thai girls!

For several years we saw her every winter during our three month stay. And then one year there came a surprise. We turned up in Chiang Mai as usual and asked Sandra over for drinks.

"I'll be right over," she said. "Can I bring my friend?"

We said of course. An hour later we were sitting on the balcony with Sandra introducing us to Francine, who was a French girl from Paris, about 40 years old. She worked at the Dhari Dhevi Hotel. We served them wine, and noticed that they used "we" a lot – as in "We are thinking of going to Bhutan in March."

So they were now a couple? It looked like it. We were surprised, but that was fine with us.

A day or so later we were able to talk to Sandra on her own, and we asked about Francine. "Yes, we are a couple", she said. "I think a lot of her and we love to travel together."

We said we were surprised but delighted. "Yes, it was a surprise. I like men, but the situation for me in Chiang Mai was not good, so I decided to consider my options, and I like girls too. I made a conscious decision to look for a female partner, and I was lucky enough to find one. You could say that I have come out!"

That was a couple of years ago. Sandra and Francine are now two of our closest friends in Chiang Mai, and I am pleased to report they are planning to get married.

16: John and Patch Fall on Hard Times

John was a friend of ours who owned a furniture factory in Hang Dong, just south of Chiang Mai. He was in his 60s and had lived in Chiang Mai for many years. His much younger Thai girlfriend was called Patcharin, but he called her Patch. They lived in a nice apartment behind the factory building, with some grounds around it. They would often invite us over for dinner, which they both helped to cook.

John made furniture under contract for hotels and apartments. Patch had the business brain, and he had the design sense. Patch was also in charge of the 'soft goods' department, where they made drapes and pillows.

I met them years before when they had a shop in the Night Bazaar. I bought a carved Thai house from them, which I still have on a table in my house in California.

But then there were political riots in Bangkok, bombs went off, and Thailand went into a depression. Hotels were no longer being built, some hotels closed, and those that remained were half empty.

No one was buying furniture for hotels and apartments, and their business dried up. They had to lay off workers, some of whom had worked for them for years. It was an unhappy time.

One person they laid off was their much-loved foreman, Natt. He was about forty years old and had a wife and two children. Before working for them, he had been a tuk tuk driver in Chiang Mai, and he reluctantly went back to that.

John and Patch rented the factory building where they also lived, and soon they were behind with the rent. Their landlord was understanding – all of Thailand was in a recession – but how much longer could this carry on?

Talking to Patch about the need to somehow get more business, I said, "Perhaps you can go to Bangkok and talk to some big hotels?"

"What about Carol Martin?" she said. Carol was a mutual acquaintance who, with her husband Justin, owned several five star hotels. John and Patch did not like to use their friendship to get business, but these were hard times, and something had to be done.

After making a very nice book of their best work in hotels and apartments in Chiang Mai, Bangkok and Phuket, Patch made an appointment for them to see Carol and Justin at their offices in Bangkok. It was kind of Carol and Justin to see them, because they had many designers and furniture manufacturers anxious for business.

"This is very good work," said Justin. "We have used you in the past and I'm sure we will again. But right now we are not building new hotels or renovating our existing ones. This is a difficult time to be in the hotel business in Thailand."

"Yes, and in our business too," said Patch.

"Leave us your photos and I will pass them along to our design team," said Justin.

Disappointed, they returned to Chiang Mai. It looked as though more layoffs would be needed, or perhaps worse. They thought about selling some land they owned near the factory.

We helped them out a little, lending them a few thousand baht, but it was really only a matter of time before the business had to close.

Then one day, they received a phone call from Carol in Bangkok.

"Hello Patch," she said. "I know you came to see us and we are sorry that we were not able to give you any business. But something has come up. We are building a hotel in Dubai and our design team is thinking of a Thai theme for some of the rooms. Would you be interested in working with us on that? They have seen your work and they think you would be perfect for the job."

"Yes, of course we would be happy to work on that!" replied Patch. "What do we need to do?"

"We want to fly you and John to Dubai to work with the designers. When can you go?"

"As soon as you can arrange it!" replied Patch.

They flew Emirates to Dubai, all expenses paid, and stayed there for a week. They worked with the designers and John took photos of the rooms. Back at their hotel he used Photoshop on his laptop to show how the rooms would look with their designs – headboards, dressers, wall coverings, drapes and lamps.

The contract covered about two hundred rooms, with most of the work being done in their factory in Chiang Mai, and eventually an installation team consisting of John, Patch, and six workers in Dubai.

But would they get the contract? Would the hotel owners trust this important work to a small company based in Chiang Mai?

We had dinner with them at their house one night, and they told us how important it was to them. "If we don't get this contract we will have to close the factory," said Patch.

They worked on pricing for a week, down to the smallest detail. Everything had to be priced in US dollars, including an ample profit margin.

Patch called me at the end of the week. "We have come up with a price," she said. "There is a lot of work to be done for two hundred rooms, but we don't want to lose the contract. We think we should charge about two million dollars. How does that sound to you?"

"That sounds a bit arbitrary", I said. "You need something that looks more like an exact amount. Also something starting with a 'one' looks a lot less than a number starting with 'two'. How about one point nine million something dollars?"

"Yes, that would be good," she replied. "The number eight is lucky, so how about one million eight hundred and eighty-eight thousand?"

"That looks like a Chinese puzzle number! Also it is too low. Try for one point nine."

"OK, we will make it … one million nine hundred and eighty eight thousand dollars. Let me talk to John about that. We will change the detail pricing so that that is the total."

Days and then weeks went by, with nothing to show. Then one day they received a call from the head of design contracting at the hotel company. "We are going to award you the contract for two hundred rooms of our new Dubai hotel," he said. "I will send you the contract for your signature."

"Thank you very much!" replied Patch. She was beside herself with excitement, and called us to celebrate.

They could not finance such a big job themselves, so they arranged for a fifty percent upfront payment on the contract. This took a couple of weeks to come through, and as soon as it did they rehired all of the laid off workers, plus a few more, and started buying materials. Patch was in charge of draperies manufacturing, and she hired several more women to help.

One day John and Patch came to see us and Patch delightedly handed us an envelope containing the few thousand baht that we had loaned them, months before.

As the furniture was made it was covered in plastic and put into large shipping containers. They were soon sending a shipping container every week off to Dubai.

The contract was a big success, and they went to Dubai to supervise the installation, which took nearly two months. Returning to Chiang Mai they considered building a house on the land that they still owned, but eventually bought a new house in Hang Dong, and quickly moved there. They hoped that after this success they would be awarded more contracts in the future.

And what of Natt, the much-loved laid off foreman? He didn't like having to go back to work as a tuk tuk driver, so he was pleased that he was the first person to be rehired. His wife was also hired as an addition to Patch's soft goods sewing team. The apartment at the back of the factory was vacant now that John and Patch had moved out, so they asked Natt and his wife and children to move in.

John and Patch are still our good friends. We are pleased that they came through their hard times, and that this story does have a happy ending!

17: Ann and Joe and the Champagne

Ann and Joe were friends of ours from Idaho. Ann was Burmese with an Indian father, and they met in Iran many years ago, when he was in the military and she was in the foreign service.

They lived in Idaho for several years, but Ann never really felt that she fit in there. After trying Penang in Malaysia for a while, they decided that they would take a look at Chiang Mai. Perhaps Thailand was the place they were looking for?

Through the Internet they found a short-term condo to rent. It was near Nimmanhaemin and owned by a German man named Hans.

They booked the condo for a month, and he asked if he could get some initial supplies for their stay. They emailed him a list of groceries, and of course they expected to pay him for this.

They arrived from Kuala Lumpur in Malaysia late one evening, and were pleased to see that Hans had arranged for a taxi from the airport, the driver holding up their name on a piece of cardboard.

Hans met them at the condo, and even put out a bottle of champagne, on ice, and two glasses, to welcome them.

"That is so kind of you!" said Joe. "Let us settle up for the groceries you bought for us."

"No need to worry about that", said Hans, "We can do that at the end of your stay."

When Hans left they considered the champagne. Although it looked expensive, Ann, being Burmese, did not drink, and Joe was more a beer drinking kind of guy. "I will see it off though", said Joe, though he never did. It sat in the cupboard until they left.

Ann and Joe had a good time during their month in Chiang Mai, and Joe made some ex-military friends by contacting the US Consulate. While they enjoyed Penang, Chiang Mai was probably more fun, and they decided that they liked Thailand more than Malaysia.

On their final day in Chiang Mai, while they were packing, Hans came over to settle up the bill.

"How did you enjoy Chiang Mai and the condo?" he asked.

"We liked both very much", said Joe, adding, "I'm sure that we will be back for a longer stay." Ann agreed with him.

"So here is the bill for the incidentals," said Hans.

Joe's chin practically hit the floor in surprise. In addition to the groceries Hans had bought for them, it listed "Taxi from the airport, 500 baht" and "One bottle of champagne, 2000 baht."

18: Dana & Bob Make a Grand Entrance

We went to the airport one day to meet our friends Dana and Bob. Actually, Dana is not just a friend but is now also my wife Sidney's stepsister. Let me tell you the story of how that happened.

Sidney met Dana when they were both in 8th grade in Turkey. Sidney's dad was in the foreign service and they lived all over the middle east, including Afghanistan, Turkey and Syria. Dana's dad was an executive with Mobil Oil, and they lived in Turkey, Colombia and elsewhere. The two families got along well, and did a lot together.

Sidney and Dana remained best friends through high school and college, through their first husbands and onto their second husbands. After many years, Dana lost her dad and Sidney lost her mom, leaving Sidney's dad and Dana's mom single and in their 80s

The two girls hatched a plot to get them together! Never say never, even if you are in your 80s! After all the years, they still liked each other, and soon the new couple, Don and Mary, were married and off to Hawaii for a honeymoon cruise.

While on the cruise, noticing their ages fellow passenger asked, "Ohh! And how long have *you two* been married?"

Mary giggled and replied, "Two days!"

So that is how, after being friends for many years, Sidney and Dana became stepsisters!

Several years later, Dana and her husband Bob were making their first visit to see us in Chiang Mai, and we excitedly drove to the airport to meet them.

There are two arrival areas at the Chiang Mai airport, domestic and international. Passengers usually fly in via Bangkok, but if they are going immediately to Chiang Mai, they can bypass customs in Bangkok. Luggage is forwarded directly to Chiang Mai to clear customs there, which is what Dana and Bob did. To meet them, we went to the International arrivals gate, just outside the customs area.

To our great surprise, we discovered that there was a red carpet, flowers, and girls in traditional pretty dresses and make up. Three monks stood to one side, one of whom looked very old. There were several army officers in uniform too. Then a brass band began to assemble, although it had not yet started to play.

We asked who was arriving, but no one who spoke English really knew. Perhaps a princess or some dignitary?

A guard opened the doors to the customs area, and the band started to play. It was a stirring moment. Just then, who should we see coming through the doors but Dana and Bob! They looked shocked to see the red carpet, the band and the welcoming monks.

"Wow, that was quite a welcome! How did you arrange that?" said Bob.

Perhaps they should have waited in the customs hall for the visiting dignitary to exit, but no one mentioned it!

Quite a grand entrance to Thailand, indeed, and we never found out who the band was for!

19: Steve and the Police Chief Make Up

Steve was a former nightclub bouncer from Birmingham, England, who now worked in security for a casino there. A bit of a 'rough diamond', he visited Pattaya two or three times a year, where he had a girlfriend named Porntip. He would often bring her to Chiang Mai for a few days, and stay at the Dusit Princess in town, in those days known as the Royal Princess.

Steve was very proud of Porntip, and would not have a bad word said about her. (Not that we would.) A former bar girl, she now worked at a restaurant in Pattaya.

One night, six of us went out to the Good View Restaurant for dinner and drinks – Steve and Porntip, Steve's friends Sue and Tony from Solihull, and my wife Sidney and I. We were going back to the Royal Princess and found an empty songthaew – the little red trucks with bench seats in the back.

Porntip went to the driver's side window to tell the driver where we were going, then quickly stepped back and announced angrily, "I am not going with this driver!"

We were shocked, and Steve asked, "What do you mean, what did he say?!"

"I not say. I don't go with this driver!" repeated Porntip.

Now Steve was angry and went over and yelled at the driver, "What the $#@% did you say to her?" The driver got out of the cab, and was clearly angry too.

There was some pushing and shoving until finally Porntip said, "He say I am bad lady. He say I should not go with farrang man!"

Steve swore loudly at the driver and after more pushing and shoving punched him hard on the chin, knocking the driver to the ground.

By now a crowd had gathered and it was best for us to pick up and leave quickly. We found another songthaew and left for the Royal Princess Hotel.

But before we got very far, the original songthaew driver pulled up alongside us, sounding his horn loudly and waving to our driver to stop. They yelled to each other in Thai, and then we set off again, the two songthaews together.

But not towards our hotel.

This didn't look good!   We drove for several minutes and pulled up outside the police station by the river. More shouting in Thai, and a police officer approached us.

With the original songthaew driver shouting and holding his face, all six of us were led inside the police station. After a short wait, we were ushered into the office of the police chief. Porntip, Steve and the driver were given seats in front of the desk, while the rest of us stood at the back of the room, trying to not get noticed.

The driver told his story to the police chief in Thai, with much holding of his bruised face. Then Porntip told her story, in Thai first and then in English, explaining that she had been Steve's girlfriend for years, and she was not a bar girl, so why was the driver so rude to her?

The police chief spoke to the driver in Thai at length, then reached over and took Steve's hand. Not to shake hands, but to hold his hand.

"In Thailand you cannot punch people," he said gently.

"Yes, but he was very rude to my girlfriend," said Steve.

"That is true, but you are a visitor here. We must be polite to you, and you must be polite to us. You cannot be angry! I would like you to apologize and shake hands with this man," the chief said, letting go of Steve's hand.

So that's what happened. Steve apologized to the driver, the driver apologized to Steve, and they shook hands. Which was unusual because the wai is more normal in Thailand.

We were relieved to not be arrested! I am not sure we have what it takes to become hardened criminals. We filed out of the police station and, with some relief, got another songthaew back to our hotel. It had been a close escape!

20: Julie and the Secret Footbridge

Riding up in the elevator to our new apartment in the Ping River Condominium one day several years ago, I shared the elevator with a young American woman who said hello and we chatted briefly. What was unusual about her was that she had a shopping cart, (which you can borrow from the building guards to carry groceries up to your apartment) and in the cart was a whole case of wine. Now, we are wine lovers ourselves, but we usually buy only two or three bottles at a time. Someone who buys wine by the case I had to meet!

We did meet in a more substantial way a couple of weeks later and we became good friends, sometimes sharing a bottle of wine in the evening on her balcony or ours. She spoke fluent Thai and became our guide to all that was best in Chiang Mai – including the restaurants and bars, even Thai restaurants where they spoke no English!

Most days she went to the gym at the D2 Hotel, and we heard that she was a Tai Chi expert, having trained in China and won an award there.

One day we saw her in the elevator and she asked us where we were going.

"To Wororot Market to buy some flowers. We like to keep fresh flowers for our Buddha!"

 "Are you going to use the footbridge?"

"Footbridge? I thought the only way to get across to the market was to use the big Nakorn Ping Bridge!"

"You don't know about the footbridge? There is a secret little footbridge. Much quicker! Walk down towards The Riverside and turn right by the little red tea house. There's a gap between the buildings, and if you walk down towards the river you will come to the footbridge."

We found the footbridge and walked across to the flower market. It was only wide enough for one person – you had to step to one side if you met someone crossing the bridge in the opposite direction. At the far end there was a plaque with the history of the bridge. Apparently, there was an earlier bamboo bridge but it had to be repaired every year because of the floods. Then in 1965, Montri Kosalphirom, a Pakistani businessman from the market, financed the new concrete footbridge in memory of his late wife, Chansom. It's actually called the Chansom Anusorn bridge (Anusorn means 'memorial' in Thai), but we always called it the Julie footbridge!

We used the 'Julie Footbridge' for several years when walking over to the flower market, or to town. But when we made our annual trip to Chiang Mai in 2011 we learned that the bridge had been damaged beyond repair when the foundation collapsed in the floods that year, and was closed for good. Both ends of the bridge were blocked off with big wooden boards. It remained in place for a couple of years but was eventually demolished.

We were sad to see the Julie footbridge go. She said that there were plans to rebuild it, "But that will never happen. This is Thailand," she said.

A year or so later, we were at our home in California and received an excited email from Julie, "You won't believe this, but they are rebuilding the footbridge! There are excavators there now. I can see it being rebuilt from my window."

We were happy to hear that. It took another year to build the bridge, and fortunately we learned that our annual trip to our Chiang Mai home would coincide with the bridge opening ceremony. It was still known as the Chansom Anusorn bridge, in memory of the original builder.

We attended the bridge opening ceremony with Julie. The ceremony was wonderful, with the usual formalities, plus children singing and dancing, monks and prayers. The whole bridge was bedecked with flags and flowers. There was a huge free picnic, including a stall from the 137 Pillars Hotel, serving our favorite pad Thai. Everyone was laughing and happy!

We crossed the bridge over to the Wororot market and bought flowers for our Buddha. We were happy to be back in Chiang Mai, and delighted that the Julie secret footbridge was back in business!

Author's Bio

Granville Kirkup is a former business and popular restaurant owner. He has been visiting Chiang Mai for almost thirty years, and has seen it change much over the years. Ten years ago he purchased a condominium in Chiang Mai, on the Ping River, and he now lives there for part of every year. He is the author of two popular Chiang Mai guidebooks. Married with two children, he lives with his wife, Sidney, in California when they are not in Chiang Mai. *Granvillekirkup2017@gmail.com*

Printed in Great Britain
by Amazon